First World War
and Army of Occupation
War Diary
France, Belgium and Germany

23 DIVISION
70 Infantry Brigade,
Brigade Machine Gun Company
1 April 1916 - 31 October 1917

WO95/2188/3

The Naval & Military Press Ltd
www.nmarchive.com
Published in association with The National Archives

Published by

The Naval & Military Press Ltd

Unit 10 Ridgewood Industrial Park,

Uckfield, East Sussex,

TN22 5QE England

Tel: +44 (0) 1825 749494

www.naval-military-press.com

www.nmarchive.com

This diary has been reprinted in facsimile from the original. Any imperfections are inevitably reproduced and the quality may fall short of modern type and cartographic standards.

© Crown Copyright
Images reproduced by permission of The National Archives, London, England, 2015.

Contents

Document type	Place/Title	Date From	Date To
Heading	WO95/2188/3		
Heading	23rd Division 70th Infy Bde 70th Machine Gun Coy. 1916 Apl-1917 Oct. To Italy.		
Heading	Attached 8th Division 70th Infy Bde 70th Machine Gun Coy. Apl - Jun 1916		
War Diary	Albert	01/04/1916	17/04/1916
War Diary	Millin Court	18/04/1916	25/04/1916
War Diary	Albert	26/04/1916	30/04/1916
Heading	War Diary Of 70th Coy Machine Gun Corps From 1st May 1916 To 31st May 1916 Volume. Vol 4		
War Diary	Albert	01/05/1916	10/05/1916
War Diary	Henencourt	11/05/1916	18/05/1916
War Diary	Millin Court	19/05/1916	21/05/1916
War Diary	Albert	28/05/1916	31/05/1916
Miscellaneous	23rd Division	30/05/1916	30/05/1916
Miscellaneous	To D.A.G. 3rd Echelon Vol I	30/06/1916	30/06/1916
War Diary	Albert	02/06/1916	04/06/1916
War Diary	Henin Court	05/06/1916	10/06/1916
War Diary	Millin Court	12/06/1916	30/06/1916
War Diary	Albert	01/06/1916	04/06/1916
War Diary	Henen Court	05/06/1916	10/06/1916
War Diary	Millen Court	12/06/1916	30/06/1916
Heading	70th M.G.C. June 1916 To Mar 18		
Heading	70th Inf. Bde. 23rd Div. Company With Bde. Rejoined From 8th Div. 17.7.16. 70th Machine Gun Company July 1916. Attached 1. Report On Action Of 1st July. 2. War Diary.		
Heading	War Diary		
War Diary	Mollens. Vidame	01/07/1916	06/07/1916
War Diary	Bruay	07/07/1916	16/07/1916
War Diary	Pollain Ville	17/07/1916	17/07/1916
War Diary	Perrogot	18/07/1916	20/07/1916
War Diary	Baizieux	21/07/1916	24/07/1916
War Diary	In The Line	25/07/1916	31/07/1916
Heading	Report On Action Of 1st July.		
Map	Report On Action Of 70th Coy M.G. Corps. On July 1st 1916 In The Assault on The Enemy Trenches 1/2 a Mile North of Ovilliers-La-Boiselle	06/07/1916	06/07/1916
Heading	70th Brigade 23rd Division. 70th Brigade Machine Gun Company August 1916		
Heading	War Diary Of To Coy M.G. Corps. August 70 M.G. Coy Vol 7		
War Diary	Fricourt	01/08/1916	07/08/1916
War Diary	Frankvillers	08/08/1916	10/08/1916
War Diary	Pont Remy	11/08/1916	12/08/1916
War Diary	Fletre	13/08/1916	13/08/1916
War Diary	Nr Steenwerck	14/08/1916	29/08/1916
War Diary	Steenwerck	30/08/1916	31/08/1916
War Diary	Steenewerck	01/09/1916	01/09/1916
War Diary	Meteren	02/09/1916	03/09/1916

Type	Location	From	To
War Diary	Wallon Cappel	04/09/1916	04/09/1916
War Diary	Clairmaison	05/09/1916	05/09/1916
War Diary	Cormette	06/09/1916	10/09/1916
War Diary	Petit Cordonette	11/09/1916	12/09/1916
War Diary	Bresle	13/09/1916	15/09/1916
War Diary	Black Wood	16/09/1916	18/09/1916
War Diary	Nr Fricourt	19/09/1916	22/09/1916
War Diary	Contalmaison	23/09/1916	26/09/1916
War Diary	Martin Puich	27/09/1916	03/10/1916
War Diary		04/10/1916	08/10/1916
War Diary	Bresle	09/10/1916	12/10/1916
War Diary	Pont Remy	13/10/1916	14/10/1916
War Diary	Argenvillers	15/10/1916	15/10/1916
War Diary	Proven	16/10/1916	16/10/1916
War Diary	Busseboom	17/10/1916	18/10/1916
War Diary	Zillebeke	19/10/1916	29/10/1916
War Diary	Poperinghe	30/10/1916	03/11/1916
War Diary	Zillebeke	04/11/1916	15/11/1916
War Diary	Poperinghe	16/11/1916	21/11/1916
War Diary	Zillebeke	22/11/1916	30/11/1916
War Diary	Ypres	01/12/1916	06/12/1916
War Diary	Brandhoek	08/12/1916	13/12/1916
War Diary	Ypres	14/12/1916	26/02/1917
War Diary	Nordausques	28/02/1917	21/03/1917
War Diary	Houtkerque	23/03/1917	05/04/1917
War Diary	Ouderdom	06/04/1917	08/04/1917
War Diary	Hill 60	09/04/1917	29/04/1917
War Diary	Ypres	01/05/1917	17/06/1917
War Diary	Meteren	17/06/1917	25/06/1917
War Diary	Ypres	26/06/1917	30/06/1917
Miscellaneous	Report On Operation Carried Out 7th June 1917. By The 70th Company Machine Gun Corps.	07/06/1917	07/06/1917
Miscellaneous	Dispositions.		
War Diary	Ypres	01/07/1917	07/07/1917
War Diary	Ouderdoom	08/07/1917	23/07/1917
War Diary	Meteren	24/07/1917	06/08/1917
War Diary	Arcques	07/08/1917	07/08/1917
War Diary	Haute Panne	08/08/1917	09/08/1917
War Diary	West Rove	10/08/1917	11/08/1917
War Diary	S. Jan. ter Biezen	12/08/1917	23/08/1917
War Diary	Busseboom	24/08/1917	24/08/1917
War Diary	Hodge	25/08/1917	01/09/1917
War Diary	Dickebusch	02/09/1917	02/09/1917
War Diary	Steenvoorde	03/09/1917	03/09/1917
War Diary	Oost-Houck	04/09/1917	12/09/1917
War Diary	Oxelaere	13/09/1917	13/09/1917
War Diary	Steenvoorde	14/09/1917	14/09/1917
War Diary	Dickebusch	15/09/1917	15/09/1917
War Diary	Hodge	17/09/1917	21/09/1917
War Diary	Ouderdoom	24/09/1917	27/09/1917
War Diary	Hodge	28/09/1917	03/10/1917
War Diary	Ridge Wood	04/10/1917	04/10/1917
War Diary	Meteren	05/10/1917	09/10/1917
War Diary	Ch Segard	10/10/1917	11/10/1917
War Diary	Wood Polygon	12/10/1917	16/10/1917
War Diary	Cn. Segard	17/10/1917	23/10/1917

War Diary	Bodmin Copse	24/10/1917	26/10/1917
War Diary	Cn. Segard	27/10/1917	28/10/1917
War Diary	West Becourt	29/10/1917	31/10/1917

No 95/2188/3

23RD DIVISION
70TH INFY BDE

70TH MACHINE GUN COY.
~~JUN 1916 - MAR 1918~~

1916 APL - 1917 OCT

TO ITALY

23RD DIVISION
70TH INFY BDE

ATTACHED 8TH DIVISION
70TH INFY BDE 23 DIV

70TH MACHINE GUN COY.
APL - JUN 1916

WAR DIARY or INTELLIGENCE SUMMARY

Army Form C. 2118.

April – June

Vol 3.5

Place	Date	Hour	Summary of Events and Information	Remarks and references to Appendices
Whit	April 1/16		Relieved 9th Bn The R Bde in the line (Kep Sector)	
"	4th		1. O.R. To Hope	
"	6th		5. O.R. Started to bay from base	
"	9th		5. O.R. To Hope	
"	10th		1. O.R. to Hope	
"	12th		1. O.R. to Hope	
"	13th		2. O.R. to Hope	
"	17th		Relieved in line by 23rd M.R. Bn by + Proceed to Millencourt + took over billets.	
Millencourt	18th		1. O.R. To Hope. 1.O.R from Hope. 44. O.R. attached for instructing in Lewis Gun	
"	19th		2. O.R. To Hope 2nd K.E. to Hawthorn. To Hope	
"	20th		1. O.R. from Hope	
"	21st		1. O.R. from Hope	
"	22nd		2. O.R. To Hope. 10.R. to from Hope. Capt J.F.F. Weirs Posted to bay from 2nd Royal Berks	
"	25th		10. R. to from Hope	

Army Form C. 2118.

WAR DIARY
or
INTELLIGENCE SUMMARY.

(Erase heading not required.)

Instructions regarding War Diaries and Intelligence Summaries are contained in F.S. Regs., Part II. and the Staff Manual respectively. Title pages will be prepared in manuscript.

COPY.

Place	Date	Hour	Summary of Events and Information	Remarks and references to Appendices
Willemeau	April 19/6/		4th O.R. attached regiment their limits	
	24/6		2 Officers 24 O.R. to Base 10 officers for further Instruction	
	25/6		20 Officers 2/4 O.R. attached from 74th Bgde of Brigade	
Albert	26/6		Rapid T.M. firing attached for Yorks. Kings	
			Relieved 2/5th in the line in the Rue Rifles Sector	
	27/6		2 O.R. Sent to enf. from Base	
	28/6		1 O.R. To Base	
	30/6		2 O.R. to Hosp.	

confidential

70 M.G Coy Vol 4

WAR DIARY.
OF.
70th Coy Machine Gun Corps.
from 1st May 1916 to 31st May 1916

VOLUME.

VIII

23

J. F. Jessop Weiss Capt
Cmdg 70th Coy. M.G. Corps.

WAR DIARY
or
INTELLIGENCE SUMMARY.

Army Form C. 2118.

Place	Date	Hour	Summary of Events and Information	Remarks and references to Appendices
Albert	1-5-16		Nil.	
"	2-5-16		1 O.R. from Hospital	
"	3-5-16		Nil.	
"	4-5-16		1 O.R. to Hospital	
"	5-5-16		1 O.R. to Hospital	
"	6-5-16		3 O.R. to Hospital	
"	7-5-16		1 O.R. from Hospital	
"	8-5-16		Nil.	
"	9-5-16		Lieut. A.L. Steel and 1 O.R. proceeded to Anti Gas school for course of instruction	
"	10-5-16		1 O.R. from Hospital. 103rd Brigade M.G. Company relieve Company in French's at 11.0 am. Company went into divisional reserve at Henencourt	
Henencourt	11-5-16		1 O.R. from Hospital. 1 O.R. attached for duties from course	
"	12-5-16		Lieut. Kirkby reforms over Must "The Puffs" struck off the strength	9 J.W. Cpt.
"	13-5-16		Lieut. J.L. De Largueril 1 O.R. to Hospital. Lieut. A.L. Steel 1 O.R. from Anti Gas School	
"	14-5-16		1 O.R. posted to Company from 6 York Lancs	
"	15-5-16		2 O.R. to Hospital	

Army Form C. 2118.

WAR DIARY
or
INTELLIGENCE SUMMARY.
(Erase heading not required.)

Instructions regarding War Diaries and Intelligence Summaries are contained in F.S. Regs., Part II. and the Staff Manual respectively. Title pages will be prepared in manuscript.

Place	Date	Hour	Summary of Events and Information	Remarks and references to Appendices
Hinencourt	16.5.16		Nil	
"	17.5.16		1 O.R. to Hospital. 1 O.R. from Hospital	
"	18.5.16		1 O.R. from Hospital	
Meaulnes	19.5.16		Returned 25th M.G.C. and became 1st Reserve to Division.	J.J.W. Capt.
"	20.5.16		1 O.R. from Hospital	
"	21.5.16		Nil	
"	22.5.16		2 O.R. to Hospital	
"	23.5.16		1 O.R. to Anti Gas School. 8 O.R. to Company from Base	
"	24.5.16		1 O.R. to Hospital 1 O.R. from Hospital	
"	25.5.16		Nil	
"	26.5.16		Nil	
"	27.5.16		Relieved 25th Bn in Trenches 8 arms to trenches S knows in Bois Rivin in Albert. 10 R from Hospital 1 o.R. from Anti Gas School	
Albert	28.5.16		Nil	
"	29.5.16		1 O.R. to Hospital	
"	30.5.16		2 O.R. from Hospital	

Army Form C. 2118.

WAR DIARY
or
INTELLIGENCE SUMMARY.
(Erase heading not required.)

Instructions regarding War Diaries and Intelligence Summaries are contained in F. S. Regs., Part II. and the Staff Manual respectively. Title pages will be prepared in manuscript.

Place	Date	Hour	Summary of Events and Information	Remarks and references to Appendices
Albert	31/5/16		French relief carried out at 9.0 am	J F J Capt.

H.Q. the
...... Division

Herewith true copies
of April & June War Diaries.
Duplicate copies of all my
War Diaries have been received
by O.C. M.G. Records London.

30/8/16

[signature]
O.C. 4th Coy M.G.C.

70 M.G Coy Vol 1

To A.G.
2nd Echelon

Herewith War Diary of
the 70th Company M.G. Corps.
for the month of June 1916

In the Field
30/6/16

J.F. Jessop-Weiss, Capt
O.C. 70 Coy M.G Corps

Army Form C. 2118.

COPY

Instructions regarding War Diaries and Intelligence Summaries are contained in F.S. Regs., Part II. and the Staff Manual respectively. Title pages will be prepared in manuscript.

WAR DIARY
or
INTELLIGENCE SUMMARY.
(Erase heading not required.)

Place	Date.	Hour	Summary of Events and Information	Remarks and references to Appendices
Albert	June 2nd	4pm	1 Officer from Hosp. 1 OR to 19mm Unit Gas School for Instruction	
"			Relieved by 23rd M.G. Coy & went into Rest at Henencourt	
"			Wood. Relieving 25th M.G. Coy. 2 Sections Kept in Billets at	
Henencourt	5th		Albert as Working Party	
"	"		1 OR Wounded	
"	6th		1 OR to Unit Gas School for Instruction	
"	7th		1 OR to Hosp. 1 OR attached 25th M.G. Coy for Instruction	
"			on various Lewis M.G. Instructors at M.G. Coy & 1 OR rejoined fr Coy	
"	10th		1 OR from Unit Gas School	
Millencourt	12n		Relieved by 23rd M.G. Coy. Relieve 25th M.G. Coy & took over	
"			Billets at Millencourt	
"	14th		1 OR to Hosp. 1 OR to Base	
"	15th		Lt & N Carte attached to Coy from 8th Y&L 2 OR rejoined fr	
"			Coy from Base 1 OR to Hosp	
"	16th		W.O. Humphrey Posted to Coy from Base 1 OR to Base	
"	17th		1 OR to Hosp. 1 OR from Hosp	

WAR DIARY
or
INTELLIGENCE SUMMARY.
(Erase heading not required.)

Army Form

Instructions regarding War Diaries and Intelligence Summaries are contained in F. S. Regs., Part II. and the Staff Manual respectively. Title pages will be prepared in manuscript.

Place	Date	Hour	Summary of Events and Information	Remarks
Mullumwe	June 18th		1 O.R. to Base	
"	19th		2 O.R. to Hosp	
"	21st		2 O.R. Party to Coy from Base. 1 2 O.R. attached to Coy as Carrying Party	
"	22nd		1 O.R. to Hosp	
"	23rd		1 O.R. to Hosp. No 2 Section Relieved 4 Regt Lynns of 25th	
"	24th		Mr & Cpl	
"	24th		1 O.R.T. to Hosp	
"	26th		2 O.R. Wounded at 19 wty	
"	29th		No 1 Section Relieved No 2 Section in Line	
"	29th		1 O.R. from Hosp. 1 O.R. Killed	
"	30th		Coy took up Position in the Trenches Previous to attack on July the 1st	

Army Form C. 2118.

WAR DIARY
or
INTELLIGENCE SUMMARY.
(Erase heading not required.)

Instructions regarding War Diaries and Intelligence Summaries are contained in F.S. Regs., Part II. and the Staff Manual respectively. Title pages will be prepared in manuscript.

Place	Date	Hour	Summary of Events and Information	Remarks and references to Appendices
ALBERT	JUNE 1916 1st		NIL	
"	2nd		2/Lt. Hawthorn rejoined Coy. from Base. 1 O.R. sent to 8th Divn anti gas school.	
"	3rd			
"	4th		Relieved by 23rd Coy M.G. Corps in trenches and proceed to HENENCOURT WOOD (under canvas) and took over billets from 25th M.G. Coy. 2 sections of Coy remain in Albert on working party of new M.G. positions. 1 O.R. slightly wounded.	
HENENCOURT	5th			
"	6th		1 O.R. from Anti-gas school. 1 O.R. to school.	
"	7th		1 O.R. to Hospital.	
"	10th		1 O.R. from Anti Gas School.	
MILLENCOURT	12th		The Company moved into MILLENCOURT and took over billets from the 25th Coy M.G. Corps.	
"	14th		1 O.R. to hospital. 1 O.R. to Base.	
"	15th		Lieut A.N. carter posted to Coy. from 8th York & Lancs. Reg. vice 2/Lt. T.G. de Longueil to U.K. sick. 2 O.R. posted to Coy. from Base. 1 O.R. to hospital.	
"	16th		2/Lt. W.O. Hampton posted to Coy. from Base. 1 O.R. to Base for dental treatment.	
"	17th		1 O.R. to Hospital. 1 O.R. from Hospital.	
"	18th		1 O.R. to Base under age	
"	19th		2 O.R. to Hospital	

WAR DIARY
or
INTELLIGENCE SUMMARY.
(Erase heading not required.)

Army Form C. 2118.

Place	Date	Hour	Summary of Events and Information	Remarks and references to Appendices
Millencourt	June 21st		2 O.R. from Base.	
"	22nd		1 O.R. to Hospital	
"	23rd		1 O.R. to Hospital. No 1 Section relieved No left guns of "25" Brigade in the line	
"	24		1 O.R. to Hospital. Heavy bombardment commenced all along our front. Section in the trenches firing 6,000 to 7,000 Rds nightly to keep enemy mine open, on Brigade front (about 500/gun)	
"	25"		Bombardment continued	
"	26"		Enemy shelled Officers billet and hit same. 2 O.R. wounded. at duty.	
"	27th		No 4 Section relieved No 2 Section in the line	
"	28		2 O.R. from Hospital. 1 O.R. Killed in action. 1 O.R. to Hospital. Remained in action. Returned to billets in Millencourt	
"	29"		went into trenches at 12 Noon. Left 1 Section No 4 in the line to keep mine open. Fired 1,000 nightly. Vic	
"	30"		1 O.R. to Hospital. No 1.2.3 Sections again move into trenches Hérissart	

J.F. Jessop Weiss
Capt 78 A.C. 7 M.G. Capt.
M.G. Capt.

70th MGC

June 1916
to Mar '18

70th Inf.Bde.
23rd Div.

Company with Bde.
rejoined from
8th Div. 17.7.16.

70TH MACHINE GUN COMPANY.

J U L Y

1 9 1 6

Attached:

1. Report on Action
   of 1st July.
2. War Diary.

WAR DIARY.

70. M.G. Coy
Army Form C. 2118.
July
Vol 6

23

1st 8th Division with
70th Brigade & rejoined
23rd Division 17.7.16.

WAR DIARY
INTELLIGENCE SUMMARY.
(Erase heading not required.)

Place	Date	Hour	Summary of Events and Information	Remarks and references to Appendices
	1916 July			
Mallano Braine	1 July		See attached summary of action taken	
"	2 "		Relieved by 56th M.G. Coy, and went by to Mollens Brotonne.	
"	3 "		Nil	
"	4 "		Nil	
"	5 "		1 O.R. from Hospital	
"	6 "		Coy entrained for Bonay	
Bonay	7 "		Took up billets in Bonay. 10 R to Hospital, 10 R from Base	
"	8 "		Nil	
"	9 "		1 O.R. to Hospital	
"	10 "		4 Gun Rotors received to replace deficiencies. 10 R from Hosp	
"	11 "		1 O.R. to Hospital	
"	12 "		2 O.R. to Hospital. 2 O.R. to Hospital	
"	13 "		2 O.R. from Base. 1 O.R. to Hospital	
"	14 "		2 O.R. to Hospital. 40 O.R. asked from Base to complete Est.	
"	15 "		2 O.R. to Hospital. 2 O.R. from Hospital	

Army Form C. 2118.

WAR DIARY
or
INTELLIGENCE SUMMARY.
(Erase heading not required.)

Place	Date	Hour	Summary of Events and Information	Remarks and references to Appendices
Bray	1916 July 16		Entrained from Bray to Amiens and marched to billets at Pollarville.	J.J.C.
Pollarville	17		Marched to billets at Parragot.	
Parragot	18		1 O.R. to Hospital	
	19		32 O.R. attached as carrying party from 70" Brigade	
	20		Nil	
	21		Marched from Parragot and took up billets in Bonjaunt	
Bonjaunt	22		Nil	
	23		Nil	
	24		2 O.R. taken from Base	
In the Line	25		Marched from Bonjaunt into Line opposite Martinpuich. N° 4 Sec. relieving one Section of N° 1 M. Gun Company. 10 R. attached manned.	
	26		1 rank wounded. 10 R. attached manned. Lieut D.E. Potter wounded.	
	27		1 O.R. from Hospital	
	28		Lieut C.A.C. Saunders posted to Coy from 69" Coy M.G.C. 1 O.R. to Hospital	

WAR DIARY
INTELLIGENCE SUMMARY.

Army Form C. 2118.

Place	Date	Hour	Summary of Events and Information	Remarks and references to Appendices
On the Line	July 1916 29th		Misc'ed [?]	J.7.J.O.
	30th		1 Officer 53 O.R. (Essex Yeomanry) 8th Hr. Gun Squadron attached. 2 O.R. to Hospital. 2 O.R. returned.	
	31st		Lieut. F. Hawthorn accidentally wounded. Lieut. C.A.E. Samson wounded, to Hospital (shell shock). Lieut. J.O. Smollie (wounded) at duty. 1 Officer 52 O.R. (Essex Yeomanry) 8th Hr. Gun Squadron ceased to be attached. Lieut. O.V. Gibson & Lieut. J.C. Gibson posted to Company from Base.	

REPORT ON ACTION OF 1ST JULY.

Report on action of 70th Coy M.G. Corps on July 1st 1916 in the assault on the enemy trenches ½ a mile North of OVILLIERS-LA-BOISELLE

Disposition
+
Instructions
Before the
assault

NO 2 Section (4 guns) in dug outs in CHORLEY St. to advance with 4th wave of left attacking battalion (8th Y+L) and to consolidate left flank up to "1st position to be consolidated".

NO I section (4 guns) in MERSEY TUNNEL position 50 yds in front of our parapet about X16a4. To fire on enemy lines + cover attacking troops as long as possible + to break through tunnel + follow troops up + consolidate 'second position to be consolidated'.

NO III section (4 guns) in ROCK street about X1a23. To fire on enemy trenches to cover advance as far as possible + then to follow troops over + consolidate right flank at 'first position to be consolidated'.

NO IV section (4 guns) two in CONNISTON street + two in BAMBERBRIDGE street to cover advance for first 25 minutes + to remain in reserve.

Second in command to cross to the enemy lines the first favourable opportunity + establish advanced Headquarters + communication with teams.

Headquarters; CONNISTON street.

Ammunition carrying party in dug out by CHORLEY Steps, to move forward to advanced Head Qrs. when ordered.

ACTION   At midnight 30th June 1st July I sent round to all sections two watches shewing Brigade time + a note that Zero time was 7.30 am. July 1st. Also I sent a note to No II Section that I thought the most favourable time for them to move was during the 4 minutes that smoke was liberated before ZERO time as I was anxious to have them in 'nomans land' before a barrage was put on our front trench. My second in command was with this section + I had a wire laid to CHORLEY street dug out which was to be eventually taken to advanced Hd Qrs.

At 7.40 am I received the following telephone message from my 2nd in command "No II Section went forward into 'nomans land' at 7.25 am

II

moved by sub-sections after 4th wave 7.30 a.m.
Good moral. 9th Y&L Bombing party just
gone forward." This I retransmitted to Brigade.

at 9.15am As I had received no orderly to report
progress I sent word to CHORLEY STEPS to find
out if any orderlies had arrived at the
ammunition dumps. The reply was that no
III Sections orderlies had just arrived + no III
section had gone forward.

at 9.40am I sent the following to Brigade "As I reported
earlier No II Section went forward with 4th
wave to secure left flank. No III section
has also gone forward. No I section has
not yet reported. I have had no report up to
time of writing from any of the sections as to
their progress in the German line. I still
hold No 4 Section in Reserve + do not propose
moving my H.Qrs + reserve section until
I hear that the other sections have progressed
+ our troops have gained the '2nd' position to
be consolidated, unless I receive orders from
you. Is this in order please?" To this B.M.
replied "approved; as far as I can make out
we are held up in the first German trench but
it is uncertain if we really hold this or not."

at 10.20am I received the following from my 2nd in command
"9.30am. Line held up in NAB. Have just
cleared front with 3 guns of no III section,
one gun out of action.. One Coy. 9th Y&L under
Lt. Thompson are now advancing." I sent
this on to Brigade.

at 10.55am the O.C. No I section personally reported to me
for instructions. He reported that he fired
from the tunnel position 6,000 rounds sweep-
ing the German front line + up towards Farm
DE MOUQUET. He had 5 men faint with
cordite fumes. He then started breaking through
the tunnel + experienced considerable difficulty,
at about 9 am he had broken out in two places.
All this time the enemy trenches were difficult
to see owing to the smoke + haze. He was
under the impression that our advance had
been a success. 2/Lt. Hampton took two guns
out + disappeared (It was afterwards found that
he + practically all the gun teams of his two guns
were killed or wounded 30 yds. from the tunnel.
2/Lt. Steel not knowing this ordered his team
out; the first 3 men were killed + the gun had
to be left a few yards away in the open. Ho the

III

stopped more men leaving & with his one remaining gun worked round to the NAB & learnt that we were not holding the German front line. His men being exhausted he put them in a dugout & reported to me for orders. I ordered him to reorganize & be prepared to collect the other gun the position of which he knew & advance when the German front line was cleared. I briefly reported this to B'Ty at

11 am. "Officer i/c. No I section reports that he has one gun left under his controls & 12 men. He suffered heavy casualties in 'no man's land'. I have given him orders to reorganize as soon as infantry advance; one other gun is recoverable from 'no man's land', the other two with an officer probably lying out in front.

at 10.45 am O.C. No II section reported on the telephone No II section from CHORLEY street dugouts got out into 'no man's land' under cover of the smoke cloud without a casualty. They advanced with the 4th line & were practically all shot down. 2/Lt Riddell being wounded. Two of the guns were in shell holes with some of the team. The remaining officer crawled back & reported; 3 men got in with him. I reported to B.Ty at

11 am. "Report from No II section. Guns in pairs are separated. Officer who reported has his two in shell hole in 'no man's land' casualties amongst men. I have ordered him to hold on & seize stragglers from Infantry to supplement for men missing and advance when first line is gained."

at about 11 am my 2nd in command reported that No III section were in the NAB. They had fired 6,000 rounds to cover advance & then had gone forward but on arriving at the NAB they grasped the situation & started engaging the enemy machine guns which were numerous & giving supporting fire to the 11th SHERWOOD Foresters who then went over. This section did remarkably good work having one gun hit in 3 places. They went on steadily keeping the enemy fire down & fired about 16,000 rounds in two hours from the NAB. Some 20 of the enemy were seen to leave his trench in a counter attack but were stopped dead by this fire. Two of the guns were pushed

IV

out into shell holes but one was too exposed & after loosing 3 men had to be withdrawn to our parapet. My second in command had seen No II section officer & was to bring his 2 guns back to assist at the NAB but this I afterwards learnt proved impossible.

at 11.7 am   I reported to Bde "No 3 section (3 guns) & No II section (2 guns) under 2nd in command have just covered advance of 11th SHERWOODS (10.55 am) who have gone over into 'no mans land'. I Coy. 9th Y&L advance covered from NAB. Guns to follow if position proves favourable."

at 11.15 am I reported to Brigade "Estimated casualties 30 OR."

at 12 noon No III section withdrew into a dug out in the NAB as there were no further troops to go over & reported this to me & asked for orders. Shortly after 12 noon my 2nd in command reported to me & I sent No III section the following order

12.50 pm   "You can only wait where you are for the present prepared for a counter attack or to consolidate any trenches we may take. 2nd in command is coming to you & you will take instructions from him. I should like to use LONGRIDGE street emplacement if available, anyhow I have given instructions to 2nd in command." I then sent my second in command back to arrange for defensive positions pending preparations for a further assault.

at 1.5 pm. I sent to Bde "6 guns missing & damaged". I now instructed No I section to attempt to recover one of the 3 missing guns. He reported

at 1.30 pm. "Enemy M.G. fire still heavy, our troops advanced on right & left" I repeated this to Brigade. He was unable to then recover the gun.

at 6. pm.   I sent to Bde "I propose organizing my Company with a view for the defence of the line. Also I propose sending out two small parties at dusk to recover the missing guns from 'no mans land'. Has this your approval?" This was approved of. When it grew sufficiently dark, I sent out two parties & 4 guns were recovered.

at about 1 am I received an order to take my company out
july 2nd   of the line. Every man made two journey's so as to leave no equipment behind which we knew

V

of.

Summary. We lost 2 guns + two guns damaged. 3 tripods missing, 1 damaged + some 70 belts + ammunition boxes missing, some of which were destroyed in a dug out which had a direct hit.

We fired 36,000 rounds from zero to 12 noon Our casualties were 2 officers + 36 O.R. The whole company did remarkably well + officers + men behaved most gallantly under very heavy fire. Lt. Munro, 2 Lt. Hawthorn + Lt. Smellie amongst the officers, Pte 22093 Sutton + Cpl 5723 Wroe amongst the men did specially good work. Their names I have sent in separately for consideration.

J. F. Jessop Weiss Capt.
cmdg 70th Coy M.G. Corps.
4/7/16

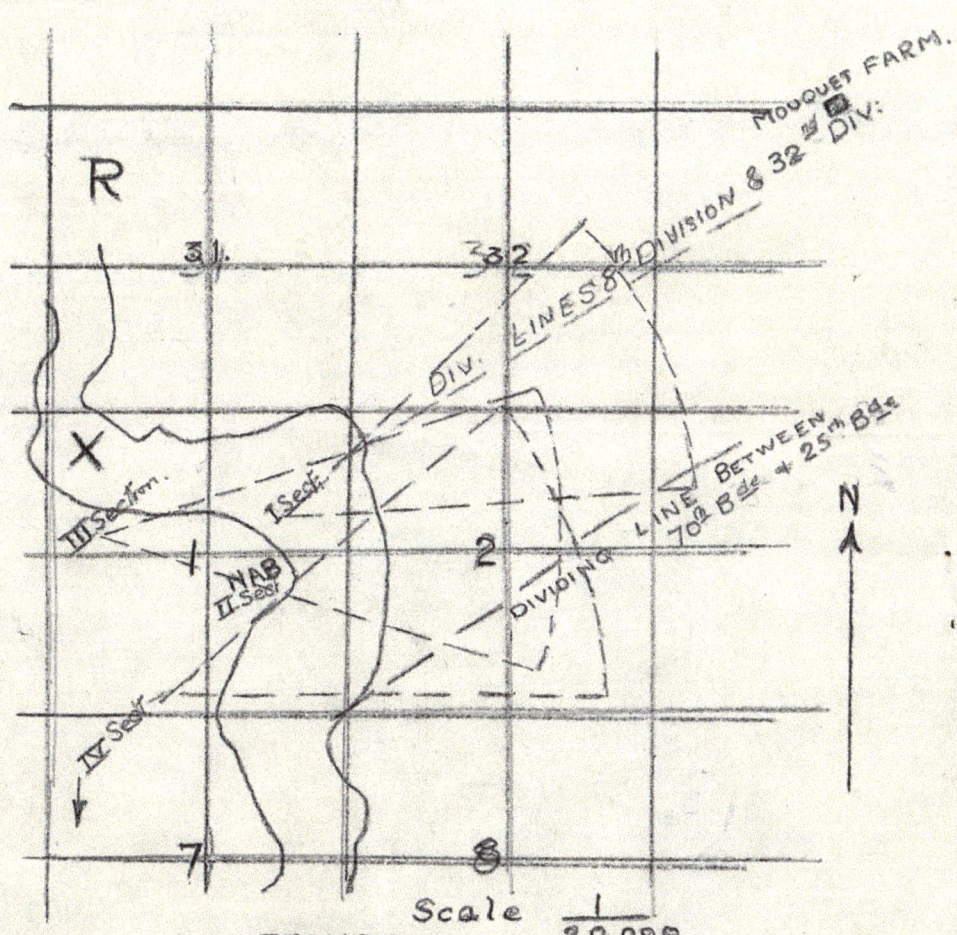

70th Brigade
23rd Division.

70th BRIGADE

MACHINE GUN COMPANY

AUGUST 1 9 1 6

70 M G Coy Vol 7

WAR DIARY
OF
70 Coy M.G. CORPS
— AUGUST —

[signature]

O.C. 70 Coy M.G. Corps

WAR DIARY or INTELLIGENCE SUMMARY

Army Form C. 2118.

Place	Date	Hour	Summary of Events and Information	Remarks and references to Appendices
Franvillers	1.8.16		2/Lt N.V. Gibson and 2 Lt F.C. Etchen posted to Coy. 2 O.R. wounded. 1 O.R. killed. 1 O.R. to hospital. 2 O.R. from hospital	
"	2.8.16		4 O.R. from hospital. 1 O.R. to hospital	
"	3.8.16		1 O.R. to hosp under age. 1 O.R. to hospital. 30 O.R. from hospital	
"	4.8.16		3 O.R. posted to Coy. 1 O.R. killed. 2 O.R. wounded. 1 O.R. to hospital. 2 O.R. from hospital	
"	5.8.16		1 O.R. to hospital. 1 O.R. from hospital. 1 O.R. wounded	
"	6.8.16		Relieved in line by 46th M.G. Coy.	
"	7.8.16		1 officer from hospital. Coy went into billets at Franvillers.	
Franvillers	8.8.16		1 O.R. from hospital	
"	9.8.16		3 O.R. to base under age. 2 O.R. to hospital. 2 O.R. from hospital	
"	10.8.16		4 O.R. posted to Coy from base. Capt. J.F.J. Weir and 1 O.R. attached H.Q. 70th Bde.	
Pont Remy	11.8.16		Coy proceeded to Pont Remy	
"	12.8.16		1 O.R. posted to Coy from base. 1 O.R. to hospital. Capt Pont Remy at 5.30 P.M. arrived at Bailleul 2.30 A.M. and went into billets at Gatre.	
Rytre	13.8.16		4 O.R. attached M.G. School Camiens for instruction. Coy took up billets near Steenwerck	
Steenwerck	14.8.16		2 M.G. Subreme Jones & Willi R. posted to Coy from base. 1 O.R. to hospital	
"	15.8.16			

Army Form C. 2118.

WAR DIARY
or
INTELLIGENCE SUMMARY.
(Erase heading not required.)

Instructions regarding War Diaries and Intelligence Summaries are contained in F. S. Regs., Part II. and the Staff Manual respectively. Title pages will be prepared in manuscript.

Place	Date	Hour	Summary of Events and Information	Remarks and references to Appendices
Nr Kemmel	16.6.16		1 O.R. to Hospital. Relieved 120th M.G. Coy in line with 12 guns.	
"	17.6.16		1 O.R. to Hospital. 1 O.R. to base under age.	
"	18.6.16		3 O.R. Hospital. 1 O.R. wounded.	
"	19.8.16		3 O.R. to Hospital.	
"	20.8.16		N.L.	
"	21.8.16		1 O.R. posted to Coy from Base. 1 O.R. from Hospital	
"	22.8.16		1 O.R. to Hospital	
"	23.8.16		1 O.R. to Base under age. 2 O.R. to Hospital	
"	24.8.16		N.L.	
"	25.8.16		3 Sections relieved in line by 69th Coy M.G. Corps	
"	26.8.16		2 O.R. from Hospital. 1 O.R. to Hospital	
"	27.8.16		N.L.	
"	28.8.16		Lieut R.G. Lorraine posted to Company from Base	
"	29.8.16		1 O.R. from Hospital. 2nd/Lt M. Carter posted to # 4 Coy M.G. Corp as 2nd in Command	

Army Form C. 2118.

WAR DIARY
or
INTELLIGENCE SUMMARY.
(Erase heading not required.)

Instructions regarding War Diaries and Intelligence Summaries are contained in F. S. Regs., Part II. and the Staff Manual respectively. Title pages will be prepared in manuscript.

Place	Date	Hour	Summary of Events and Information	Remarks and references to Appendices
Shorncliffe	Aug. 30th		1 O.R. from Hospital	
	31st		4 transport Drivers posted to Coy. from Base. 2 O.R. from Hospital.	

A.V.Munn. Lieut
for O.C. 40th Cdn. D.A.C. Corps.

Army Form C. 2118

WAR DIARY
or
INTELLIGENCE SUMMARY.
(Erase heading not required.)

70th Machine Gun Coy

Place	Date	Hour	Summary of Events and Information	Remarks and references to Appendices
	Sept. 1916			
Shewmenck	1st		One O.R. to Hospital. Left Shewmenck q arrived in billets at Ytrehram	
Ytrehram	2nd		Nil.	
do	3rd		Left Ytrehram q arrived in billets at Wallon Calfell. One O.R. to Hospital	
Wallon-Calfell	4th		Left Wallon Calfell q arrived in billets at Clairemaison.	
Clairemaison	5th		Left Clairemaison q arrived in billets at Cornette.	
Cornette	6th		Nil	
do	7th		Three O.R. from Hospital	
do	8th		Nil	
do	9th		Nil	
do	10th		Left Cornette q arrived in billets at Petit Cordonette.	
Petit Cordonette	11th		Two O.R. to Hospital q one O.R. from Hospital.	
do	12th		Left Petit Cordonette q arrived in billets at Breule.	
Breule	13th		Nil.	
do	14th		Three O.R. from Hospital. One O.R. to base.	
do	15th		One O.R. to Hospital. Lt. A.R. Munro to England authority IX corps wire A593 dated 10th Sept 1916. Lt. A.S. Edwards M.G. 15th Bn & buy posted to this coy. authority IX corps wire	

Army Form C. 2118.

WAR DIARY
or
INTELLIGENCE SUMMARY.
(Erase heading not required.)

Instructions regarding War Diaries and Intelligence Summaries are contained in F. S. Regs., Part II. and the Staff Manual respectively. Title pages will be prepared in manuscript.

Place	Date	Hour	Summary of Events and Information	Remarks and references to Appendices
Bresle	September 15th 1916		Left Bresle and arrived at BLACK WOOD near ALBERT	9.1.E
BLACK WOOD	16th		NIL	
"	17th		NIL	
"	18th		One O.R. from Hospital. Left Camp at ALBERT and went into Divisional Reserve near FRICOUR[T]	
N. FRICOURT	19th		NIL	
"	20th		NIL	
"	21st		1. O.R. to Base	
"	22nd		1. O.R. to Hospital and relieved 68th M.G. Coy in support at CONTALMAISON.	
CONTALMAISON	23rd		1. O.R. to Hospital	
"	24th		1. O.R. from Hospital	
"	25th		1. O.R. wounded at Duty	
"	26th		Relieved 68th M.G. Coy in line at MARTINPUICH. 2 Sections in line and 2 in support	
MARTINPUICH	27th		NIL	

WAR DIARY
or
INTELLIGENCE SUMMARY.

(Erase heading not required.)

Army Form C. 2118.

Place	Date	Hour	Summary of Events and Information	Remarks and references to Appendices
MARTINPUICH	September 28th	1916	1 O.R. to Hospital	
"	29th		2nd Lieut. P. TAYLOR wounded; Two O.R's killed, Two O.R. Wounded	
"	30th		Two O.R. wounded; Two O.R Hospital	

Arthur W Tuttle
5-10-16

9.9 Warwic Regt
Comdg 10th Batt
W of Capt^s

Original.

Army Form C. 2118.

Vol 9

Instructions regarding War Diaries and Intelligence Summaries are contained in F.S. Regs., Part II. and the Staff Manual respectively. Title pages will be prepared in manuscript.

WAR DIARY
or
INTELLIGENCE SUMMARY.
(Erase heading not required.)

Place	Date	Hour	Summary of Events and Information	Remarks and references to Appendices
Foncquevillers	October 1916 1st & 2nd		Took part in an action by 91st Infantry Brigade taking two lines of trenches at Les Sars. The following were casualties in action: two Officers wounded; One O.R. killed; Seventeen O.R. wounded; One O.R. missing.	
"	3rd		Relieved by 69th M.G. Coy in the line. Proceeded to billets near Foncquevillers in Divisional Reserve.	
Acheux	4		Six O.R. to hospital; One O.R. from hospital.	
"	5		One O.R. to hospital;	
"	6		One O.R. to hospital;	
"	7		Twenty O.R. posted from base	
"	8		Three O.R. from hospital;	
"	9		Lieut B.B.H. Druitt & 2nd Lt. G.B.O. Gorman posted from base; Two O.R. from hospital	
"	10		Ten O.R. posted from base	
"	11		Nil	
"	12		Left Acheux & entrained from Albert to Pont Remy;	
Pont Remy	13		Ten O.R. posted to Coy from base;	
"	14		Left Pont Remy & proceeded by road to Argenvillers;	

Original

Army Form C. 2118.

WAR DIARY
or
INTELLIGENCE SUMMARY.
(Erase heading not required.)

Instructions regarding War Diaries and Intelligence Summaries are contained in F. S. Regs., Part II. and the Staff Manual respectively. Title pages will be prepared in manuscript.

Place	Date	Hour	Summary of Events and Information	Remarks and references to Appendices
	October 1916			
Ingouville	15		Left Ongouville & entrained at St Riquier for Proven.	
Proven	16		Arrived in camp at Buysscroom	
Buysscroom	17		Nil	
"	18		Relieved 4th Australian M. G. Coy in the line at Zillebeke; two sections in the line; one in support at Ypres; one in reserve at Buysscroom.	
Zillebeke	19		One O.R. to hospital.	
"	20		Two O.R. evacuated & struck off strength of company.	
"	21		One O.R. from hospital	
"	22		Nil	
"	23		No 3 section relieved by No 1 section in the line; No 2 section relieved by No 4 section	
"	24		Nil	
"	25		One O.R. to hospital	
"	26		Nil	
"	27		Nil	
"	28		Two O.R. to hospital. The company relieved by No 68 M.G.C. in the line	
"	29		Arrived in billets in Poperinghe	

Original

Army Form C. 2118.

WAR DIARY
or
INTELLIGENCE SUMMARY.

(Erase heading not required.)

Instructions regarding War Diaries and Intelligence Summaries are contained in F. S. Regs., Part II. and the Staff Manual respectively. Title pages will be prepared in manuscript.

Place	Date	Hour	Summary of Events and Information	Remarks and references to Appendices
Popéringhé	October 1916 30		One O.R from hospital	
"	31		Two O R to hospital	

A S Edwards Lt
for O/c 70 Coy M.G.C.

Army Form C. 2118.

70th Coy M.G. Coy

Vol 10

WAR DIARY
or
INTELLIGENCE SUMMARY.
(Erase heading not required.)

Place	Date	Hour	Summary of Events and Information	Remarks and references to Appendices
	November			
Poperinghe	1st		Seven OR to hospital. 1 Officer leave.	
"	2nd		1. O.R from Hospital. 1 Officer to Hospital.	
"	3		1. O.R to Hospital. Relieved 89th Coy. M.G.C. in the line	
Zillebeke	4		2. O.R to Hospital. 1 O.R from Hospital.	
"	5		1. O.R from Hospital	
"	6		1. O.R to Hospital. Lieut. Walker attached 1st Divisional Bayonet School.	
	7		O/Came M.g. Robert Carried for instructional purposes. C.S.M reported sick	
	8		NIL	
	9		3. O.R from Hospital	
	10		2. O.R leave. 1 O.R from Hospital	
	11		1. O.R to Hospital. 1 OR from Hospital	
	12		2. OR to Hospital	
	13		NIL	
	14		Corpl Hardie attached 1st Divisional Grenade School	
	15		1. O.R to Hospital	
	16		1 OR to Hospital. Relieved in the line by 68 Coy M.G.C.	

Poperinghe

WAR DIARY or INTELLIGENCE SUMMARY

Army Form C. 2118.

70th Coy M.G. Corps.

Place	Date	Hour	Summary of Events and Information	Remarks and references to Appendices
POPERINGHE	17		2 O.R. from Hospital. 2 O.R. leave.	
	18		1 O.R. from Hospital	
	19		1 O.R. to Hospital	
	20		Capt. Harding rejoined from Grenade School	
	21		1 O.R. on leave. Rehearsal 89th Coy. M.G.C. attd. Zone. 1 O.R. from Hospital. 1 O.R. proceeds on leave	?/4/17
ZUIDPEENE	22		NIL	
	23		NIL. 2/Lt E.D. Wilson from entrainment of leave. 23 Div. G 1649/94	
	24		NIL	
	25		2 O.R. from leave. 6 came rejoins from M.G. School. 1 O.R. on leave.	
	26		NIL	
	27		33 O.R. from Infantry 70th Inf. Bde. Transferred to M.G. Coy to bring up gun teams from 6 OR to 8 OR. 1 OR from Hospital	
	29		13 OR to Base being surplus to establishment	
	30		2 O.R. posted from Base. 2/Lt. WADSWORTH reported for duty from Base.	

G.H. Weir
O.C. 70th Coy M.G. Corps.

Army Form C. 2118.

Vol II

70th Coy M.G. Corps

WAR DIARY
or
INTELLIGENCE SUMMARY.
(Erase heading not required.)

Instructions regarding War Diaries and Intelligence Summaries are contained in F. S. Regs., Part II. and the Staff Manual respectively. Title pages will be prepared in manuscript.

Place	Date	Hour	Summary of Events and Information	Remarks and references to Appendices
YPRES	1.12.16		2 O.R. to Hospital. 2/Lt L.D. Gosling posted to Company from Base	
"	3.12.16		1 O.R. to Hospital	
"	4.12.16		4 O.R. to Hospital, 1 O.R. from Hospital	
"	5.12.16		1 O.R. to Hospital, 1 O.R. from Hospital	
"	6.12.16		Relieved in trenches by 68th Company, proceeded to Bks Braddock	E.F.7
Braddock	8.12.16		2 O.R.'s to Hospital	
"	9.12.16		1 O.R. to Hospital	
"	10.12.16		1 O.R. to Hospital	
"	11.12.16		1 O.R. to Hospital	
"	13.12.16		8 O.R.'s to Hospital	
YPRES	14.12.16		Relieved 69th Company in Ythan Left Sector	
"	16.12.16		2 O.R.'s from Hospital; 2 O.R.'s rejoined from M.G. School Camiers	
"	20.12.16		1 O.R. from Hospital, 1 O.R. to Hospital	
"	22.12.16		1 O.R. to Hospital	
"	24.12.16		1 O.R. from Hospital	
"	25.12.16		1 O.R. from Hospital, 1 O.R. to Hospital	

Army Form C. 2118.

WAR DIARY
or
INTELLIGENCE SUMMARY.
(Erase heading not required.)

Place	Date	Hour	Summary of Events and Information	Remarks and references to Appendices
YPRES	26.7.16		Lieut J.W.B. Carsonから Company から Base. 1 Officer + 20 O.R's to CAMIERS.	9.1/3.
	27 "		10.R. from Hospital. 20 R's to Hospital	
	28 "		10.R. to Hospital	
	29 "		10.R from Hospital - 10.R hosted for Base. 10.R. Wounded	
	30 "		10.R. from Hospital	
	31st		NIL	

J.F.J. Westmoreland
Comdg 70th Coy M.G. Corps.
3/1/17.

Vol 1   Army Form C. 2118.

70th Machine Gun Coy

WAR DIARY
or
INTELLIGENCE SUMMARY.
(Erase heading not required.)

Place	Date	Hour	Summary of Events and Information	Remarks and references to Appendices
YPRES	Jan'17 1st		3 ORs to Hospital	
	2		1 OR to Hospital	
	5		1 Officer evacuated, sick.	
	6		1 OR to Hospital 1 OR from Hospital	
	7		Relieved 69th M.G. Coy in its Right Section.	
	10		1 OR to Hospital	
	11		1 OR to Hospital	
	12		1 OR to Hospital	
	14		1 OR from Hospital	
	15		1 OR to M.G. School 2 OR from M.G. School	
	16		Lieut. E.V. RANDALL posted to Coy from Base	
	18		1 OR to Hospital	
	19		1 OR to UK 2 OR to Hospital	
	20		1 OR wounded	
	21		5 OR to Hospital	

Army Form C. 2118.

WAR DIARY
or
INTELLIGENCE SUMMARY.
(Erase heading not required.)

Place	Date	Hour	Summary of Events and Information	Remarks and references to Appendices
YPRES	Jan/17			
	22		2 O.R. from Hospital	
	24		3 O.R. from Hospital	
	27		1 O.R. to Base Depôt	
	28		1 O.R. from Hospital	
	29		1 O.R. from Hospital	
	30		2 O.R. from Hospital	
	31		Relieved the 69th Coy M.G.C. in the left sector	Relieved by the 68th M.G. Coy in the Right Sector.

A.S. Edwards Lt
O/C 70th M.G.C.

Army Form C. 2118.

WAR DIARY
or
INTELLIGENCE SUMMARY.
(Erase heading not required.)

70th Machine Gun Coy

Y/MR/13

Place	Date	Hour	Summary of Events and Information	Remarks and references to Appendices
YPRES	February 1917			
	3rd		1 O.R. to Base	
	5th		1 O.R. to Base Depot. 1 O.R. from M.G. School	
			2/Lt M.Y. Gibson and 1 O.R. to M.G. School.	
	6th		1 O.R. to Hospital	
	8		1 O.R. to Hospital	
	10		1 O.R. to Hospital 2/Lt S.A. Parkes posted from Base Depot	
	13		1 O.R. from Hospital	
	15		1 O.R. from Hospital 1 O.R. to Hospital	
	16		Relieved by 68th M.G. Coy in the left sector	
	19		2 O.R. to Base Depot	
	22		1 O.R. from Hospital	
	24		2 O.R. to U.K. Relieved by 116th M.G. Coy in Capa Posen Proceeded by train to MERCKEGHEM.	
	25		Left MERCKEGHEM. Proceeded by road to BAYENGHEM	
	26		Left BAYENGHEM. Proceeded by road to NORDAUSQUES.	
NORDAUSQUES	28		2/Lt M.Y. Gibson and 1 O.R. rejoined from M.G. School. 1 O.R. to 4th Scottish General Hospital from leave.	

Army Form C. 2118.

WAR DIARY
or
INTELLIGENCE SUMMARY.
(Erase heading not required.)

70th Machine Gun Coy

Place	Date	Hour	Summary of Events and Information	Remarks and references to Appendices
NORDAUSQUES	1.3.17		1 O.R. to Hospital	
"	2.3.17		1 O.R. to Hospital.	
"	6.3.17		1 O.R. to Hospital.	
"	7.3.17		Lieut. E.A. Dowman. to M.G.T.C. (Cavalry). Auth. A&Q A/8659 D/4/3/17	
"	10.3.17		1 O.R. to Hospital. 1 O.R. from Hospital.	
"	16.3.17		1 O.R. to Hospital.	
"	16.3.17		1 O.R. from Hospital.	
"	9.3.17		Lieut. E.W. Randall to Hospital. Left Nordausques (proceed)	
"			by road to Bayenghem.	
"	20.3.17		Left BAYENGHEM proceeded by road to MERCKEGHEM. 1 O.R. from Hosp.	
"	21.3.17		Left MERCKEGHEM proceeded by road to HOUTKERQUE.	
HOUTKERQUE	23.3.17		1 O.R. to Hospital.	
"	25.3.17		1 O.R. to Hospital.	
"	27.3.17		Lieut. E.W. Randall from Hospital	
"	30.3.17		Lieut. J.W.A. Parsons to Hospital.	
"	31.3.17		1 O.R. to Hospital.	

Army Form C. 2118.

Vol 75 — 70th Machine Gun Coy

WAR DIARY
or
INTELLIGENCE SUMMARY
(Erase heading not required.)

Instructions regarding War Diaries and Intelligence Summaries are contained in F. S. Regs., Part II. and the Staff Manual respectively. Title pages will be prepared in manuscript.

Place	Date	Hour	Summary of Events and Information	Remarks and references to Appendices
HOUTKERQUE	April 3		1 O.R. to Hospital	
	4		1 O.R. from Hospital	
	5		Marched from HOUTKERQUE to Camp near OUDERDOM	
OUDERDOM	6		1 Officer from Hospital. 1 O.R. to Hospital. 3 O.R. from the Base.	
	7		2 O.R. to Hospital	
	8		1 Section relieved 1 Section of 4th M.M.G. Batt. in Hill 60 Sub-sector	
HILL 60	9		2 O.R. wounded. Relieved 142 M.G. Coy. in Hill 60 Sub sector	
	10		1 O.R. from Hospital.	
	13		1 O.R. to Hospital. 1 Officer to M.G. Course at CAMIERS	
	15		1 O.R. to Base Depot, under age. 1 O.R. leave to U.K.	
	16		Relieved by 69th M.G. Company in Hill 60 Sub Sector. 2 Sections relieved 2 Sections of 68th M.G. Coy	
			1 O.R. to Hospital.	
			on A.A. duty at ABEELE.	
	17		1 O.R. to Hospital	
	19		2 O.R. join to Company from Base	

Army Form C. 2118.

WAR DIARY
or
INTELLIGENCE SUMMARY.
(Erase heading not required.)

Instructions regarding War Diaries and Intelligence Summaries are contained in F.S. Regs., Part II. and the Staff Manual respectively. Title pages will be prepared in manuscript.

Place	Date	Hour	Summary of Events and Information	Remarks and references to Appendices
	March			
	19		2 O.R. from Hospital	
	21		Capt J.O. Cook 20th County of London Regt. attached for instruction	
	23		2 Section relieved 2 Section of 69th M.G. Coy in Hill 60 Sub-sector.	
			2 O.R. to Hospital	
	24		C.S.M. Parish 5703 granted 1 month leave to U.K. on re-engaging to complete 21 years	
			2 O.R. posted to Company from Base	
			2 Section relieved at Argue by 69th M.G. Coy	
	25.		Relieved 69th M.G. Coy in Hill 60 Sub-sector. 1 O.R. from Hospital	
	26		2. O.R. returned from leave.	
	28		3. O.R. to Hospital 4 O.R. from Hospital	
	29		2 O.R. to M.G. School Camieres.	

C.S.H. Smith Lieut & Adjt
70th Coy M.G.C.

Army Form C. 2118.

WAR DIARY
or
INTELLIGENCE SUMMARY.
(Erase heading not required.)

Instructions regarding War Diaries and Intelligence Summaries are contained in F.S. Regs., Part II. and the Staff Manual respectively. Title pages will be prepared in manuscript.

70th M.G. Co.
Vol 16

Place	Date	Hour	Summary of Events and Information	Remarks and references to Appendices
YPRES	May 1917			
	1st		Relieved by 57th M.G.Coy in Ave 60 Sector	
	2nd		2 O.R. posted to Coy. from Base. 1 O.R. from Hospital	
	3rd		2 O.R. from Hospital	
	4th		1 O.R. from Hospital	
	5th		2 O.R. to Hospital	
	7th		1 O.R. to Hospital	
	8th			
	9th		Capt J.W. Smallman posted to Coy. from Base.	
	10th		2 O.R. to Hospital. 2 O.R. to Hospital	
	11th		Left Boeschepe Area & arrived at Winnipeg Camp	
	12th		Relieved 58th M.G. Coy in the line Left Sector	
	14th		Capt J.O. Cook wounded at Duty. 2 O.R. to Hospital	
	15th		2 O.R. to Hospital. Relieved in the line by 72nd M.G. Coy. Proceeded to Billets at Montreal Camp	
	16th		Left Montreal Camp & arrived in Boeschepe Area	
	17th		1 O.R. from Hospital	

Army Form C. 2118.

WAR DIARY
or
INTELLIGENCE SUMMARY.
(Erase heading not required.)

Place	Date	Hour	Summary of Events and Information	Remarks and references to Appendices
YPRES	May 1917			
	19th		1 O.R. from Hospital	
	20th		2 O.R. rejoined from M.G. School Camieres	
	21st		1 O.R. to Hospital	
	22nd		32 O.R. attached as carrying parts from 8th York & Lancs. Regt.	
	23rd		1 O.R. to Hospital	
	24th		2 O.R. to Hospital. Relieved 69th M.G. Coy in Hill 60 Sector	
	26th		1 O.R. from Hospital. 2 O.Rs to Hospital	
	27th		Capt J.L. Coer to Hospital	
	28th		1 O.R. wounded in action. 1 O.R. from Hospital. 1 O.R. to Hospital	
	29th		3 O.R. wounded (2 still duty)	
	30th		2 O.R. to Hospital	

WAR DIARY or INTELLIGENCE SUMMARY

Army Form C. 2118.

70th Coy M.G.C.

JUL 17

Place	Date	Hour	Summary of Events and Information	Remarks and references to Appendices
YPRES	June 1917			
	1st		Relieved by 68th Coy M.G.C. in the line Hill 60 Sector	1 O.R. killed in Action
	2nd		1 O.R. from Hospital	
	3rd		Capt. J.O. Cook from Hospital	
	5		Company proceeded to the Trenches to take up positions in the Mount Sorrel Sector attached "Report on Operations" which see also for the 6th and 7th	
	6		6 O.Rs posted to Company from Base	
	7		Lieut C.W. RANDALL to Hospital	
	8th		5 O.R. Killed in Action Lieut L.D. GOSLING and 10 O.R wounded	
	9		Capt. J.W. SMALLMAN and 2 O.Rs returned from M.G. School Camiers	
			3 O.R. killed & 4 O.Rs wounded 1 O.R. wounded at H.Q.	
	11th		Capt. J.O. Cook 20th London Regt attached to establishment	
	13th		2 O.R. from Hospital	
	14th		1 O.R. to Hospital 11 O.Rs posted to Company from Base	
	16		5 O.Rs to Hospital	
			Relieved in the line by 15=72nd M.G. Coy and proceeded to Billets at METEREN	
	17th		Capt. J.O. SMALLMAN to Base Depot Lieut A.S. EDWARDS M.C. appointed to	

Army Form C. 2118.

WAR DIARY
or
INTELLIGENCE SUMMARY.
(Erase heading not required.)

Instructions regarding War Diaries and Intelligence Summaries are contained in F. S. Regs., Part II. and the Staff Manual respectively. Title pages will be prepared in manuscript.

Place	Date	Hour	Summary of Events and Information	Remarks and references to Appendices
METEREN	JUNE 1917			
	17th		To command 70th M.G. Coy dated 11th June 1917. 2nd Lt H.M JENKINS 2nd Lt G.A. ALLAN 2nd Lt S.G. MOODY appointed and 2.3. O.R. posted to Company from Base Depot.	
	20th		6 O.R. to Hospital	
	21st		1 O.R. to Hospital	
	22nd		2 O.R. from Hospital	
	23rd		3 O.R. from Hospital	
	25th		1 O.R. from Hospital. 1 O.R transferred to 69 Coy M.G.C. 1 O.R. transferred to 68 Coy M.G.C Lieut C.E.H DRUITT appointed Second in Command, dated 11th June 1917	
	26th		Left METEREN & arrived in Buffs C at RENINGHURST	
YPRES	28th		Relieved 17th Coy. M.G.C. in the Mount SORREL Sector. 10 guns in the line and 6 guns & 191 M.G. Coy in reserve	
	29th		1 O.R to Hospital	
	30th		1 O.R wounded 1 O.R joined company from Base	O.R. Strike list to Coy to Coy Coy of 3.7.17

Army Form C. 2118.

WAR DIARY
or
INTELLIGENCE SUMMARY.
(Erase heading not required.)

Place	Date	Hour	Summary of Events and Information	Remarks and references to Appendices
			The following were the Awards for gallantry and devotion to duty during the operations covering 7th to 9th June 1917	
			Lieut A.S. Edwards, MC — Bar to M.C.	
			Lieut N.Y. Gibson — M C	
			5729 Sgt. H. Maloy — D.C.M.	
			5730 L/Cpl A. Bashford — D.C.M.	
			26635 Pte A Ward — Military Medal	
			5757 Pte R Barr — M.M	
			42025 Pte S. Bowden — M.M	
			35128 L/Cpl J Baldwin — M.M	
			62769 Pte J Phillips — M.M	
			34238 Pte J Robson — M.M	

REPORT ON OPERATIONS

Carried out 7th June 1917.

By the 70th COMPANY MACHINE GUN CORPS.

CONTENTS.
-0-0-0-0-0-0

Page. No. 1.	DISPOSITIONS.
ditto.	ADMINISTRATIVE ARRANGEMENTS.
Page No. 2.	PLAN OF ATTACK.
Page No. 3.	"THE ATTACK".
Page. No. 4.	LESSONS.

DISPOSITIONS.   PAGE 1.

Para.1. Disposition for Attack on the night 6th/7th June.
No.3 Section assembled in MOUNT SORREL SUBWAYS attached to the 9th Battn York & Lancs Regt.
2.Guns of No.4 Section assembled in MOUNT SORREL SUBWAYS attached to the 8th York & Lancs Regt.
No.2.Section assembled in HEDGE STREET SUBWAYS attached to the 11th Sherwood Forresters.
2.Guns of No.4 Section assembled in CRAB CRAWL SUBWAYS attached to 8th K.O.Y.L.I.Rsgt.
No.1 Section in RESERVE at CRAB CRAWL SUBWAYS defending the LEFT FLANK.
Company Hqrs CRAB CRAWL SUBWAYS.

Para.2. Method of ASSEMBLY.
On the night of the 4th/5th June No.2 Section moved into HEDGE STREET SUBWAY.   No.1 Section Relieved 194 Company in OBSERVATORY RIDGE.
On the night of the 5th/6th No.3 Section moved to MOUNT SORREL. 1/2 No.4 Section moved to MOUNT SORREL, and 1/2 to CRAB CRAWL. Company Headqrs moved to CRAB CRAWL.
At 9.a.m. on the 6th No.1 Section moved from OBSERVATORY RIDGE to CRAB CRAWL.

ADMINISTRATIVE ARRANGEMENTS.

Para 1. The following DUMPS were formed:-

    a) MOUNT SORREL Subways.
    b) HEDGE STREET Subways.
    c) ZILLEBEKE.

At A. & B. the DUMPS were formed as follows:-

1.Sergt. & 7.Men
16.Gallons of Water.   1.Drum Oil.
20.Belt Boxes.   10,000 Rds S.A.A.
1.Belt Filling Machine.

At "C" there were 40,000 Rds S.A.A. and Reserve Rations and Water in charge of the C.Q.M.S.

Para.2. 40.Men were attached from the Infantry to act as Carriers & Personnel at the DUMPS.

The following was the method of carrying:-
No.1 The Tripod.
No.2. Gun, Spare Parts, & Spare Barrel.
No.3. Condenser, and 3.Belt Boxes.
No.4. 4.Galls Water.
No.5. 3.Belt Boxes & Shovel.
No.6. & 7. 3.Belt Boxes each.

The last 2.Men were the Infantry Carriers.

Each Man also carried
2.Sandbags.
2.Mills Bombs.
24.Hours Rations
1 Iron Ration.
Full Water Bottles.
1. Shell-Dressing.

Each Officer had with him his Servant & 1 Orderly.

PLAN OF ATTACK.   PAGE 2.

Para.1.   FIRST OBJECTIVE.

On the First Objective being taken No's 2.& 3.Sections were to move over and help Consolidate.
Section Officers were to use their own discretion as to when they could move, Zero plus 1.Hour being given as an Approximate Time.

No.2 Section was to take up roughly the following Positions:-
- 1.Gun at I.30.b.15.15.
- 1.Gun at I.30.d.2.5.
- 1.Gun in proposed Strong Point at MOUNT SORREL I.30.c.6.9.
- 1.Gun at I.30.b.50.55.

This Section was to defend the LEFT FLANK and to prevent the Enemy from forming up in SHREWSBURY FORREST in order to Counter attack.

No.3 Section was allotted Positions as follows:-
- 2.Guns in IMMEDIATE SUPPORT (1.Gun in proposed Strong Point at I.30.c.60.35.)
- 2.Guns in IMAGE RESERVE.

Para.2.   SECOND OBJECTIVE.

On the Second Objective being taken No.4 Section were to move over, 2 Guns in support of K.O.Y.L.I.Regt., and 2.Guns in support 8th York & Lancs Regt.
Zerp plus 5.Hours was given as an Approximate Time.
2. of these Guns were to be employed between I.36.b.50.75. & I.36.b.0.3., 1.being used to cover the KLEIN ZILLEBEKE RD. & the KNOLL to the EAST of it, and the other in a Strong Point at I.36.a.7.8.
The other 2.Guns were to take up Positions between I.30. d.25. & I.36.b.50.75.

Para.3.   THE RESERVE SECTION.

No.1 Section had 4.Shafts from the CRAB CRAWL Subways, Commanding the LEFT FLANK, which they could Man in the event of a Counter Attack.

Para.4.   The Ground was reconnoitred before-hand as far as possible by Officers & N.C.Os.
This was fairly easily accomplished in the case of the LEFT SECTOR by making use of the 5wp SAPS "F" & "G".

"THE ATTACK" PAGE. 3

Ref: ZILLEBEKE TRENCH MAP 1/10,000.

Zero Hour 3.10.a.m. 7th June

1st OBJECTIVE.

LEFT SECTOR.

At Zero plus 60.Minutes No.2 Section went over in Support of the 11th Sherwood Forresters. Owing to the Smoke and general excitement three Teams lost Direction, and suffered heavy Casualties, by going too far North of the Objective. The Section Officer and One Gun Team were knocked out going across "No Man's Land".
One Gun arrived at its Objective at I.30.d.2.5., and the other two Guns took up Positions in the German Front Line at the junction of IMAGE TRENCH and ILLUSIVE TRENCH, so as to Defend the Left Flank against any possible Counter Attack.

RIGHT SECTOR.

At Zero plus 45.Minutes No.3 Section went over in support of the 9th Battn York & Lancs Regt.
Two Guns took up Positions in IMMEDIATE SUPPORT; One of these came into Action against some 30.of the Enemy as they attempted to Retire.
Two Guns lost direction, and were found supporting the Left Battalion (11th Sherwood Forresters).
One of these Guns was left in Position at I.30.d.3.4 to Strengthen the Left Flank, this leaving One Gun Firing to-wards "CLONMEL COPSE", and another in a South Westerly Direction.
The other Gun was removed to IMMEDIATE SUPPORT, and took up a Position at I.30.c.60.35.

2nd OBJECTIVE.

At 8.30.a.m. two Guns of No.4 Section went over in support of the 8th Battn York & Lancs Regt, and arrived in IMMEDIATE SUPPORT. One Gun was sent up to a Position at I.36.b.3.9., and the other stayed in IMMEDIATE SUPPORT till Dusk, when it was taken to a Position a 100.Yards in Front of our New Line to cover THE KNOLL and the KLEIN ZILLEBEKE ROAD about I.36.b.1.4.
Of the Two Guns in support of the 8th K.O.Y.L.I.Regt One was held in Reserve in IMMEDIATE SUPPORT and the other was sent up to the Front Line, and took up a Position at I.30.d.55.05.

At Zero plus 9.Hours the Enemy, estimated strength about 250. Men, Counter-Attacked on the Left from the Direction of CLONMEL COPSE.
They were seen massing, and the Four Guns on Crab Crawl came into Action in their Shaft Positions immediately.
The Three Guns in support of the Left Battalion also came into Action, and accounted for a considerable number of the Enemy as they came across.
The Enemy entered our Front Line, but was unable to stay there for more than 15.Minutes owing to very heavy Machine Gun

Machine Gun And Rifle Fire.   Between 30. & 40 were left dead in the Trench, besides those Killed on the way across and the way Back.
The Enemy had evidently intended to stay, as Machine Guns accompanied the Infantry who came across with Picks & Shovels with instructions to Dig.

The Night of the 7th/8th was fairly quiet.

ADMINISTRATIVE.

One Central DUMP was formed in IMMEDIATE SUPPORT, the two DUMPS A. & B being abolished.
The following Stores were sent up on the Night of the 7th/8th and the following Night:-
    20. Belt Boxes.
17,000 Rds S.A.A.
    24. Galls Water.
  2. Belt-filling Machines.
  2. Drums Oil.

LESSONS LEARNT.

The Method of Carrying, and the Supply of Ammunition and Water was quite satisfactory.
The chief lessons to be learnt seem to be the following:-

1. Machine Guns should go over with the last attacking wave of the Infantry, so as not to lose Direction, and to ensure reaching their Objectives.   If the Infantry has not gained their Objective, it would be seen in time and the Guns would not go over.   The advantages of this are that they would get over quickly before any Heavy Barrage could be directed on them, that they would be concealed, and that they would have a better chance of keeping Direction.

2. The Personell of a Machine Gun Company is inadaquate.
40. Additional Men are required to make it Self-Supporting in Action.

WAR DIARY or INTELLIGENCE SUMMARY

Army Form C. 2118.

90th Machine Gun Company Vol 18

Place	Date	Hour	Summary of Events and Information	Remarks and references to Appendices
YPRES	1.7.17		2 O.R's wounded, 2 O.R's Hospital	
"	2.7.17		1 O.R to Hospital, 1 O.R killed in Action	
"	3.7.17		6 O.R's posted to the Company from the BMGC	
"	7.7.17		Relieved by 58th Machine Gun Company Hill 60 Sector. 2 O.R's to Hospital	
DUG OUT DOOM	8.7.17		Captain J.O. Cork transferred to 219th Machine Gun Company. 5 O.R.S Hospital. 6 Company from Rest.	
"	9.7.17		2 O.R's killed in Action. 4 O.R's wounded	
"	10.7.17		2 O.R's to Hospital	
"	12.7.17		1 Section relieved 1 Section of 194 Company in Chateau Hill 60 Sector. 1 O.R to Hospital	
"	13.7.17		4 O.R's wounded in Action. 1 O.R to Hospital	
"	14.7.17		2 O.R's to Hospital. 2 O.R's from Hospital	
"	15.7.17		Lieut. N. V. GIBSON M.C. wounded. 1 O.R to Hospital	
"	16.7.17		4 O.R's to Hospital	
"	17.7.17		1 O.R killed. 2 O.R's wounded, 1 to Hospital Sick.	

Army Form C. 2118.

WAR DIARY
or
INTELLIGENCE SUMMARY.   70th Machine Gun Company
(Erase heading not required.)

Place	Date	Hour	Summary of Events and Information	Remarks and references to Appendices
OUDEZEM	19.7.17		1 O.R. wounded. 1 O.R. to Hospital Sick. 4 O.R's from Hospital.	
"	20.7.17		1 O.R. to Hospital	
"	22.7.17		2nd Lieut. H.J. Ward posted to Company from Reel	
"	23.7.17		Left OUDERDOM & proceeded by road to METEREN AREA.	
METEREN	24.7.17		2nd Lieut. T.F. McGREGOR posted to Company from Reel. 1 O.R. from Hospital	
"	25.7.17		1 O.R. to Hospital	
"	26.7.17		1 O.R. to Hospital, 2 from Hospital	
"	28.7.17		Lieut. C.E.H. DRUITT & 2 O.R. attached to M.G. School, CAMIERS. 4 Officers & 4 O.R's with eight guns returned to M.G. Company in the Anti-Aircraft Cordon at ABEELE	
"	30.7.17		1 O.R. to Hospital	
"	31.7.17		1 O.R. attached to No. 22 Vet. Hospital ABBEVILLE.	

A.S. Echren? Capt.

Army Form C. 2118.

70ᵗʰ Company M.G.C.

Vol 19

WAR DIARY
or
INTELLIGENCE SUMMARY.
(Erase heading not required.)

Instructions regarding War Diaries and Intelligence Summaries are contained in F.S. Regs., Part II. and the Staff Manual respectively. Title pages will be prepared in manuscript.

Place	Date	Hour	Summary of Events and Information	Remarks and references to Appendices
METEREN	2.8.17		I.O.R. from Base Depot. I.O.R. from A.H.T.D. 2 O.R's rejoined from Divisional Gas School.	
"	4.8.17		I.O.R. rejoined Company from Base. 2/Lt S.G. Moody to Hospital (sick)	
"	6.8.17		Left METEREN and entrained at CAESTRE for ARCQUES	
ARCQUES	7.8.17		Left ARCQUES and proceeded by march route to HAUTE PANNE. I.O.R. transferred to Base Depot.	
HAUTE PANNE	8.8.17		2/Lt W.H. Wadsworth struck off strength. (Authy G.M.G. No D/1921 dated 5.8.17)	
"	9.8.17		Left HAUTE PANNE & entrained at WIZERNES. 2 O.R. rejoined Company from Base. 2 O.R's from Hospital & 2/Lt S.G. Moody from Hospital.	
WESTROVE	10.8.17		3 O.R's attached to 23' Division M.G. School.	
"	11.8.17		Left WESTROVE & entrained at WATTEN for PROVEN. Went to Lekke at Sᵗ JAN-ter-BIEZEN.	
S JAN-ter BIEZEN	12.8.17		2/Lt S.G. Moody transferred to 229ᵗʰ Company. (Authy G X Corps No 2118/60/23 dated 3.8.17)	
"	13.8.17		2/Lt T.F. McGregor admitted to Hospital	
"	14.8.17		2/Lt H. Ward attached to 18ᵗʰ Corps School for Instruction. I.O.R. to Hospital. 2 I.O.R. rejoined from Base.	

Army Form C. 2118.

70th Company M.G.C.

WAR DIARY
or
INTELLIGENCE SUMMARY.
(Erase heading not required.)

Instructions regarding War Diaries and Intelligence Summaries are contained in F.S. Regs., Part II. and the Staff Manual respectively. Title pages will be prepared in manuscript.

Place	Date	Hour	Summary of Events and Information	Remarks and references to Appendices
S¹ JAN-tel-DIEU	18.8.17		2/Lt H Ward rejoined from 18th Corps School. 3 O.R's rejoined from 23rd Div. M.G. School. 1 O.R from A.H.T.D.	
"	23.8.17		Capt S¹ Jn. Le - Queger turned at BUSSEBOOM.	
BUSSEBOOM	24.8.17		2/Lt R.J. Fitzgerald posted to Company.	
HOOGE	25.8.17		7th Company went into the line. HOOGE Sector & relieved the 41st & 42nd M.G. Company. 5 O.R's Killed and 5 O.R wounded ; 1 O.R wounded at Duty.	
			2 O.R attached wounded.	
"	28.8.17		1 O.R killed. 4 O.R's wounded.	
"	29.8.17		2 O.R wounded.	
"	30.8.17		1 O.R from Base Depôt + 12 O.R posted to Company from 19 S'MG Coy	
"	31.8.17		Relieved by 7 M.S. Coy went into Barrage Position at HOOGE & Headquarters proceed killed at DICKEBUSH.	

A S Edwards Capt
Commanding 70th Coy M.G.C.

Army Form C. 2118.

90th Coy M.G.C.

VI 20

WAR DIARY
or
INTELLIGENCE SUMMARY.
(Erase heading not required.)

Place	Date	Hour	Summary of Events and Information	Remarks and references to Appendices
HOOGE DICKEBUSCH	1.9.17		Relieved in Clines by the 7th Machine Gun Company + went & billets at DICKEBUSCH	
DICKEBUSCH	2.9.17		Left DICKEBUSCH + marched to billets in STEENVOORDE Area.	
STEENVOORDE	3.9.17		Left STEENVOORDE + marched to OOST-HOUCK.	
OOST-HOUCK	4.9.17		11 O.R. posted from Base	
"	5.9.17		2/Lt W.J DEVT + 6 O.R. posted to Company from Base.	
"	6. "		10 O.R. posted to Company from Base.	
"	10. "		2 Officers + 25 O.R. attached to 2nd Division	
"	11. "		Lt L.W.A. PARSONS struck off Company strength (ADV27/SB/4 of 17.) Authority	
"	12. "		Left OOST-HOUCK + moved in billets at OXELAERNE	
OXELBERG	13 "		Left OXELAERNE + moved to STEENVOORDE. 2/Lt E.L MARSHALL posted to Company from Base.	
STEENVOORDE	14 "		Lt STEENVOORDE + moved at DICKEBUSCH. Lt. T.E.H. DRUITT transferred to 140 M.G Coy (Lt Command) Authority 10 Coph No 2118/20 23a. 2 O.R. posted to Coy from A.H.T.D. 2 section returns to the lines	11.9.17
DICKEBUSCH	15th "		9.17 M.G Coy to the Reserve House SECTOR. 2 Section moved to BRIELT at OUDERDOM.	

Army Form C. 2118.

WAR DIARY
or
INTELLIGENCE SUMMARY.
(Erase heading not required.)

70th Bde. M.G.C.

Place	Date	Hour	Summary of Events and Information	Remarks and references to Appendices
HOOGE	17.9.17		1 O.R. wounded.	
"	18." "		2/Lt H.J. WARD + 10 O.R. wounded	
"	19." "		Relieved in the line by 69th M.G. Coy + went to barrage	
"	" "		positions (to support attack on the 20th)	
"	" "		2/Lt E.L. MARSHALL + 4 O.R. wounded	
"	21.9.17		1 O.R. wounded + 12 O.R. posts to Contact from Bns. 72 By.	
"	"		4 wounded from the went into billets at DUDGEROOM	
DUDGEROOM	24.9.17		Left DUDGEROOM went to Hallebast Corner.	
			2/Lt R. OWEN, 2/Lt E. SPDNEY, 2/Lt H. HARRIS	
			joined Company from Base. 3 Officers + 50 O.R. attached	
			to 23" Division for duty work.	
	26.9.17		3 officers + 60 O.R. rejoined from 23" Division	
	27." "		Relieved the 70th Bde 1.4 in the line HUGE CRATER.	
HOOGE	28.9.17		Details + transport arrived at DICKIE BUSH.	
"	29."		1 O.R. to M.S. 6 Lt. COMIERS, 1 O.R. from Hoy. Self. (Ampiers).	
			4 O.R. wounded + 6 O.R. to Hospital gas poisoning.	
"	30.9.17		4. O.R. to Hospital (gas)	

A Ebraed Capt.
Commanding 70th By M.G.C.

Army Form C. 2118.

70 Coy. M.G.C.

Vol 21

WAR DIARY
or
INTELLIGENCE SUMMARY.
(Erase heading not required.)

Instructions regarding War Diaries and Intelligence Summaries are contained in F.S. Regs., Part II. and the Staff Manual respectively. Title pages will be prepared in manuscript.

Place	Date	Hour	Summary of Events and Information	Remarks and references to Appendices
HOOGE CRATER	1.10.17		3. O.R. to Hospital	
"	2.10.17		3. O.R. to Hospital	
"	3.10.17		1. O.R. to Hospital. Relieved by the 13th M.G. Coy. in the line.	
RIDGEWOOD	4.10.17		Proceeded to BILLETS at METEREN	
METEREN	5.10.17		4 O.R. to Hospital. 4 O.R. posted to Company from Base Depot. 2 O.R. from Hospital	
"	6.10.17		1 O.R. from Hospital	
"	7.10.17		" Lt. A.C. BREWITT joined Company as 2nd in Command	
"			from 23rd Coy.	
"	8.10.17		1 O.R. posted to Company from Base.	
"	9.10.17		Left METEREN + arrived at CHATEAU SEGARD. 1 O.R. to Hospital	
CH. SEGARD	10.10.17		1. O.R. to Hospital	
"	11.10.17		2/Lt G. Cahn + 2/Lt H.M. JENKINS to Hospital	
			Relieved the 23rd M.G. Coy in the line POLYGON WOOD.	
WOOD POLYGON	12.10.17		4. O.R. to Hospital	
"	13.10.17		1. O.R. to Hospital. Lt. A.L. STEEL wounded at duty. 1. O.R. wounded	
"	14. "		1 O.R. to Hospital. 1 O.R. wounded	

Army Form C. 2118.

WAR DIARY
or
INTELLIGENCE SUMMARY. 70th M.J.C.
(Erase heading not required.)

Instructions regarding War Diaries and Intelligence Summaries are contained in F. S. Regs., Part II. and the Staff Manual respectively. Title pages will be prepared in manuscript.

Place	Date	Hour	Summary of Events and Information	Remarks and references to Appendices
POLYGON WOOD	13.10.17		1. O.R. killed, 1 O.R. wounded	
"	18.10.17		" 1 O.R. to Hospital	
Ct. SECARD	19.10.17		Lt A.L.C. PEEL attached 2nd in Command of 10th M.J. Coy. Relieved by 69th M.J. Coy in line. 2 O.R. of to Hospital	
"	19 "		1 O.R. to Hospital. 4 O.R. joined Coy from dem.	
"	19.10.17		2 O.R. to Hospital	
"	20.10.17		1 O.R. to Hospital	
"	21.10.17		2 Sections 70 Coy attached to 69 M.J. Coy + 2 Sections of 69 M.J. Coy attached to 70th Coy. 2 O.R. joined to Coy from dem.	
"	22.10.17		70 Coy less 2 sections attached to 7th Division. 1 O.R. to Hospital	
"	22 "		1 O.R. to Hospital	
"	23.10.17		1 O.R. to Hospital. Relieved Ch 119 Siege Battery ODDM & COPSE	
ODDM COPSE	24.10.17		2 Officers posted to Coy from dem. 2/Lt G.R. Maurice + 2/Lt F.A. GORDON	
"	25.10.17		1 O.R. wounded at duty.	
"	26.10.17		Relieved by the 22nd M.J. Coy. 1 O.R. to Hospital	
Ct. SEGARD	27.10.17		Commenced utility lines to WESTHOEK CORNER. 2 Section rejoined from 69 Coy.	
Ct SEGARD	28.10.17			

T1134. Wt. W708-776. 500,000. 4/15. Sir J. C. & S.

Army Form C. 2118.

WAR DIARY
or
INTELLIGENCE SUMMARY.   TO GOC
(Erase heading not required.)

Instructions regarding War Diaries and Intelligence Summaries are contained in F. S. Regs., Part II. and the Staff Manual respectively. Title pages will be prepared in manuscript.

Place	Date	Hour	Summary of Events and Information	Remarks and references to Appendices
WESTOUTRE Sq.28.a.7				
"	30/10/17		2/Lt F. G. Jordan to Hospital	
"	31/10/17		I.O.Q. to Hospital.	

Osmond Capt
O. boy 70 Company
Machine Gun Corps

www.ingramcontent.com/pod-product-compliance
Lightning Source LLC
Chambersburg PA
CBHW081240170426
43191CB00034B/1991